Original title:
Berry Bush Ballads

Copyright © 2025 Creative Arts Management OÜ
All rights reserved.

Author: Maya Livingston
ISBN HARDBACK: 978-1-80566-711-7
ISBN PAPERBACK: 978-1-80566-996-8

The Enchanted Hush

In the garden, whispers grow,
Bouncing berries in a row.
All the critters come to play,
Chasing shadows, what a day!

The squirrels dance with such delight,
While frogs jump high to take their flight.
Each giggle echoes through the trees,
As honeybees buzz 'round with ease.

Tip-toe through that bramble patch,
Watch your step, there's quite a catch!
A cheeky rabbit grins and hops,
Just as the springtime laughter pops.

Berries bouncing off my nose,
As the fragrant chaos grows.
Every mishap brings a cheer,
In this funny, wild frontier.

Delights Among the Leaves

In a thicket, full of fun,
Berries glitter like the sun.
Chickadees join the joyous spree,
Singing songs of jubilee.

A bear dons a berry crown,
While raccoons giggle, tumbling down.
Nature's playground, full of glee,
Every nook a mystery!

Ants march proudly in a line,
With tiny treats, their favorite wine.
A snail plays tag, oh what a sight!
As we dance till the fall of night.

Caterpillars wear a scarf,
While grasshoppers joke and laugh.
This leafy laughter never fades,
In our whimsical escapades.

Odes to Nature's Offerings

Gather 'round, hear this tale,
Of berries bright, we will regale.
Crimson jewels, like dropped stars,
In the field, near old rusty cars.

A pig in boots comes to explore,
With a plump berry stuck to its snore.
A parade of joy, each critter struts,
While skunks do cartwheels in their ruts.

Nature's feast, such a sight,
With silly dances, pure delight.
Every flavor, a playful tease,
And laughter floats upon the breeze.

Berries spilled from my clumsy hands,
A cheeky raccoon takes its stands.
Oh laughter, how you twirl and spin,
As we chase the joy within!

Envelopes of Essence

In a patch where berries roam,
Nature gifts a sweetened home.
Butterflies swirl in dizzy flight,
As autumn leaves swirl in delight.

A jester fox, with wild appeal,
Juggles berries like a meal.
Tumbling down, they roll and bounce,
Joining in the joyful flounce.

Wobbling owls in the moonlight glow,
Offer wisdom, but don't you know?
How to giggle when things go wrong,
In this raucous, berry-song!

A dance of flavors, wild and free,
With laughter spilling like a sea.
From every nook and cranny, cheer,
In this playful land, we hold dear.

The Aroma of Solitude

In the garden where silence talks,
Sneaky raccoons in striped socks.
They nibble fruit and dance around,
Oh, what a sight in the quiet sound!

A squirrel hops with a cheeky grin,
Chasing shadows, it's sure to win.
It sniffs the air, so sweet and bold,
While hiding treasures, oh so old.

Sun sets low, with a wink so sly,
As crickets chirp a lullaby.
The sweet aromas drift and play,
In this peaceful, silly ballet.

Clusters of Joy

Laughter bounces all around,
As friends gather upon the ground.
With baskets full of laughter bright,
Filling hearts with pure delight.

A duck waddles, quacks with glee,
Joining in, how can it be?
They share their snacks, a berry feast,
While storytelling, the joy increased.

Oh, in this patch of colors fair,
Every berry a vibrant affair.
With each sweet bite, they giggle loud,
Creating memories, so unbowed.

Tranquil Tresses

In the meadow where hairpin bends,
Mischievous winds play with the friends.
Each tuft of grass, a gentle twirl,
As time slows down; oh, what a whirl!

Butterflies flutter, donning hats,
While bees buzz in the midst of chats.
Flower crowns in wild disarray,
All join the fun in their free play.

A tumble here, a twirl up there,
Laughter spills like sweetened air.
With every twist, the joy ignites,
In tranquil tresses, pure delight.

Ripe Reflections

Mirrors crack in the sweet sun's glow,
With friends who dance, and twirl, and throw.
Each berry plucked holds a giggle bright,
In every smile, the world's just right.

The pond reflects the joyful noise,
Water rippling with their poise.
A frog joins in with a silly jump,
Creating splashes, oh what a thump!

In ripe reflections, friends unite,
Painting the day with colors bright.
Together they find in simple glee,
Life's sweet moments, wild and free.

Sweetness Wrapped in Green

In the garden, laughter blooms,
Beneath the leaves, a dance of grooms.
A plump red fruit, does it giggle?
Watch it wobble, oh what a wiggle!

All the critters come to play,
Chasing shadows through the day.
Jelly jars in sunlit rows,
Who could resist such tasty shows?

Frost-Kissed Petals of Rebirth

When winter slips, the sun peeks through,
Dewdrops shimmer, a morning cue.
Petals blush, a shy hello,
But watch those bees, they steal the show!

As springtime throws a leafy prank,
The blooms all gather by the bank.
They giggle as they start to tease,
The bumblebees buzz with such ease!

A Symphony of Seasonal Picks

See the basket, a colorful feast,
With fruity symphonies, joy increased.
The pickers are singing with laughter loud,
While the fruit gets saucy, feeling proud!

Pecked by the sparrows, cheeky and sly,
"Is this for us?" they flap and fly.
The fruits just roll, not wanting to be,
The next great dish for Grandma's spree!

Shimmering Jewels Among the Leaves

Among the leaves, the treasure glows,
A little sparkle where no one knows.
A squirrel swoops, with his twitchy tail,
Sings a song of summer's trail!

The berries laugh, ripe on the vine,
"Pick me first!" they call, so divine.
As the sun dips low, casting its rays,
The garden's encore steals the gaze!

Portraits of the Hidden Orchard

In an orchard where the fruits dance,
A squirrel pranks, he takes his chance.
With acorn hat and cheeky grin,
He steals my snacks, then runs to win.

Under trees with tangled roots,
The rabbits wear their funny boots.
They hop around, a silly sight,
In search of berries, day and night.

The apples giggle, plump and round,
While pears make jokes, a silly sound.
Peaches blush, so ripe and sweet,
All join in for a fruity feat.

With laughter shared among the leaves,
Each hidden laugh the joy achieves.
The orchard sings in bright delight,
Where every fruit's a comic sight.

Reflections in the Juicy Meadow

In the meadow, bright and green,
Grasshoppers dance, a lively scene.
They wear their hats, a tad too high,
While butterflies all float and fly.

Daisies giggle at the bees,
Who buzz around with absent ease.
They stop to chat, then get distracted,
By flowers' jokes, so well enacted.

Frogs on lilypads, with flair,
Croak out tunes, light as the air.
They sing to frogs, who sing along,
Their chorus weak but oh so strong.

With juicy fruits and tasty treats,
The meadow hums, as nature greets.
Each reflection sparkles bright,
In this garden, pure delight.

Crimson Harvest

The sun is out, a radiant glow,
Through vines and leaves, the laughter flows.
Tomatoes wear their red, proud capes,
As children trip, in silly scrapes.

Pumpkins laugh from their cozy place,
With round, fat faces, all in grace.
They roll around, they want to play,
In harvest fun, they steal the day.

Carrots peek from the soil bed,
While radishes dance on tiny tread.
With roots that wiggle and dance about,
They cheer for veggies, there's no doubt.

In baskets full of color bright,
The harvest brings a joyful sight.
Each fruit and veggie, potluck cheer,
Makes every bite a laugh sincere.

Whispers of the Thicket

In the thicket, secrets hide,
Where raccoons joke, their eyes so wide.
With masks of mischief, they play tricks,
While owls hoot, with clever picks.

Berries giggle, soft and sweet,
They roll around, what a treat!
The blackbirds chirp, a funny tune,
At nighttime dances, under the moon.

Foxes tread with silent glee,
While fireflies light a blinky spree.
Rabbits hop, with twinkling eyes,
In nature's joke, laughter flies.

Amidst the whispers, soft and low,
The thicket hums with ebb and flow.
Each petal, leaf, and critter's cheer,
Makes every moment feel so near.

Beneath the Overhanging Canopy

Under the leaves, a giggle spins,
Blushing fruit where mischief begins.
Squirrels conspire, plotting a snack,
While birds above share tales of a hack.

A plump raspberry wears a crown,
Upon a throne, it won't back down.
The elders laugh, the young ones cheer,
As ants parade like they own the sphere.

Hidden treasures all around,
Cherries chuckle without a sound.
A bumblebee's dance is quite the jest,
While the nervous snail fails the speed test.

In twilight's glow, the creatures jive,
As wild whims and witticisms thrive.
With every nibble and every squawk,
Nature's comedy is quite the talk.

Hymns of the Hidden

Where shadows linger, secrets dwell,
A chorus of giggles, you can't quite tell.
Plump blueberries share a sly glance,
While the sunflowers sway in a silly dance.

Nature's choir sings out loud,
Ripe laughter wrapped in a leafy shroud.
The fox in the brush giggles with glee,
As critters convene for a fruit jamboree.

Under the thorns, a shy little sprout,
Dreams of the day when it'll break out.
Oh, the tales it will tell from the ground,
With each berry's grin, hilarity found.

When evening falls, the stars ignite,
The harvest moon shines, oh what a sight!
Whispers of laughter dance through the trees,
As all join in for a night of ease.

The Language of Thorns

In a vineyard wild, nonsense is spry,
Where vines weave stories that tickle the sky.
Raspberry rants and blackberry sighs,
Silent thorns laugh, stealing the prize.

A playful crow with a berry stew,
Sips from the cup of the morning dew.
While ladybugs giggle on low-hanging leaves,
Plotting their heists, oh what a thieves!

Amid the greenery, wise owls conspire,
To spread the tales of thorny attire.
Who wore the most vibrant, who stole the scene?
A riot of colors, the grandest routine.

And so they chatter through whispers and cheer,
About berry boogies throughout the year.
With every harvest, hilarity grows,
A language of laughter where anything goes.

Ripened Echoes

In a garden lush with ripened delight,
Pineapple piñatas swing in the night.
Watermelons joke with their juicy cheer,
As friends gather 'round, the laughter is near.

Strawberries blushing, shy but bold,
They spill the secrets that they've been told.
While unlikely pals dance on the ground,
An epic show where joy is profound.

The gossip flows like nectar sweet,
As squirrels debate 'bout their favorite treat.
A blueberry busts out with a pun,
Fruits cracking jokes as they bask in the sun.

Through evening's glow, the echoes ring,
Ripened fruits join in for a vibrant fling.
With laughter cascading like a stream,
This garden of giggles is pureest dream.

Dew-kissed Dreams

In the morning bright and early,
A raccoon wears a shirt so pearly.
He dances round with berries red,
While singing tunes inside his head.

The squirrels gather, quite a show,
With acorn hats, they steal the grow.
Each giggle echoes through the trees,
As berries tumble in the breeze.

A strawberry slips and accidental,
Causes chaos; it's fundamental!
As creatures tumble, giggles soar,
In dew-kissed dreams, we crave for more.

Just watch the antics of this crew,
With sneaky plans they all pursue.
For in this garden, life's a treat,
As laughter dances with our feet.

Chants of the Wild

The fox in boots sings loud and proud,
While prancing 'neath a fluffy cloud.
The berries sing and join the tune,
While dancing 'round a big old moon.

A bear with shades, so cool and bright,
Comes waltzing in, he's quite a sight!
He sways and twirls, oh what a feat,
With berry juices on his feet!

The nightingale, a bard so sly,
Picks up the mic; he's such a guy!
His voice cascades through leafy halls,
As creatures gather, breaking walls.

Each critter joins in, wild and free,
With berry hats, as happy as can be.
Through laughter fills the vibrant night,
In chants that make the stars ignite!

The Thicket's Lullaby

In the thicket, critters snore,
While dreams of berries gently pour.
A sleepy hedgehog hums away,
In cozy nooks where shadows play.

An owl with pillow on his head,
Sings softly as the sun turns red.
The baby bunnies bounce in dreams,
As rumbles echo with berry themes.

In berry beds where mushrooms sway,
The critters dream of sunny days.
A lullaby of laughter bright,
Where sweet adventures take their flight.

So close your eyes and drift along,
With whispers of the thicket's song.
For in this land of sleepy sighs,
We feast on dreams — a sweet surprise!

Vibrations of the Vines

The vines are jiving, what a scene,
With dancing berries, oh so green!
A band of bugs with tiny horns,
Play tunes of ripeness 'til the morns.

A chubby rabbit wears a scarf,
And hops along to make us laugh.
With every step, he wobbles, sways,
A bouncing ball of joy ablaze.

The grapes are grooving, swaying low,
While berry tunes make summer glow.
As critters join in wild delight,
The vines vibrate, holding tight.

So grab a friend, let's twist and twirl,
With berry jams, watch laughter swirl!
For in this patch of fun divine,
We celebrate the vibes — so fine!

Songs of the Summer Thicket

In a thicket lush and bright,
The critters dance with pure delight.
A squirrel sings, a rabbit prances,
While bees in tune join their glances.

The sunbeams bust a joyful move,
Even ants in line find their groove.
A jolly frog croaks out a rhyme,
Declaring it's a berry-picking time!

The bushes giggle, leaves can't pause,
A chorus swells, from nature's jaws.
A song of sweet, a melody rife,
Enticing all to join this life.

As spiders spin their web of cheer,
They weave the sounds for all to hear.
With every rustle, every gleam,
In this thicket, life's a dream!

Nectar's Flirtation with the Breeze

A flower flirts with breezy sway,
It teases bees to come and play.
With every blush, it calls them near,
"Come sip my joy, my nectar dear!"

The wind, a matchmaker, glees,
Whispers sweet nothings through the leaves.
"Play nice, oh blooms, don't be so shy,
Let every petal catch the eye!"

The butterflies, in fancy dress,
Join in the fun, never less.
With laughter lilting on the air,
They find romance without a care.

When twilight hums its soft refrain,
The dance resumes—oh, what a gain!
For in this swirl of twinkling light,
Nature's flirts are pure delight!

Vibrant Melodies from the Thorns

In thorny thickets, laughter grows,
Where every creature steals the show.
A hedgehog strums on a twig so fine,
While berries bob in rhythm divine.

A porcupine plays a wooden flute,
"Oh, tune me up, let's all hoot!"
With each note, a flower sways,
And everyone hums through the sunny days.

Amidst the tangles, stories weave,
As cheeky birds gather and cleave.
They wish to rival the band so merry,
But can't resist a snack of cherry!

As thorns applaud, they hold their breath,
Waiting for nature's warm, sweet depth.
With every echo, joy expands,
In this vibrant show, life takes a stand!

The Secret Life of Fruity Branches

Hidden high, in leafy dreams,
The branches giggle in sunny beams.
"Who would think we're such a blast?
A fruity party, hold on fast!"

Elderberries tell a cheeky joke,
As citrus laughs till their sides choke.
The apples wink, it's sweet and tart,
Together they make a juicy art.

"Let's have a brawl, a berry squish!"
Cried the grapes, "It's our fruity wish!"
With loads of pinks, and oranges bright,
The branches dance in sheer delight.

And as the stars begin to gleam,
Those fruity pals unite and beam.
With secrets shared and smiles in bunches,
The night becomes a feast of crunches!

Lullabies of the Woodlands

In the woods where critters play,
Squirrels dance the night away.
While owls hoot a silly tune,
Balloons float beneath the moon.

Frogs perform a splashy show,
Kangaroo hops, but oh so slow.
The trees giggle with a breeze,
Chasing giggles through the leaves.

A raccoon wearing a cute hat,
Tells jokes to the sleepy cat.
A lullaby of rustling leaves,
As nighttime wraps and softly weaves.

So lay your head and take a rest,
The woodland's humor is the best.
Beneath the stars, the laughter flows,
In this dream where joy just grows.

Enchanted Flora

In the garden, flowers prance,
With petals bright, they seem to dance.
The daisies munch on chocolate cake,
While tulips giggle, wide awake.

Buttercups play peek-a-boo,
With bumblebees that hum a tune.
The violets wear their brightest smiles,
As daisies flaunt their quirky styles.

A daffodil cracks up in glee,
Telling tales of wobbly bees.
The roses share their funniest news,
And spin the tale of rainbow hues.

So wander through this flower patch,
Where laughter blooms; oh what a catch!
In every leaf and in every stem,
The jokes are shared, again and again.

Luscious Notes from the Underbrush

In the thicket where the wild things sing,
A fox juggles berries, what a thing!
Badgers chuckle at the scene,
As raccoons start a pie cuisine.

A hedgehog plays a tiny flute,
While squirrels drum on hollow fruit.
The underbrush holds a merry show,
With roots that wiggle to and fro.

A chortle from the bushes spry,
As fireflies twinkle in the sky.
The blackberry laughs as it falls,
And bounces back, oh how it sprawls!

So come and join this woodland fest,
Where nuts and berries laugh the best.
With every nibble, take a chance,
And join the critters in their dance!

Sunkissed Whispers

Under the sun where shadows play,
The dandelions twirl in ballet.
A snail recites a humor verse,
While butterflies joke, which is worse?

The sunflowers toss their heads in glee,
Competing for the silliest spree.
The daisies snicker, "Who's the best?"
As ladybugs join in the jest.

The day unfolds with chuckles loud,
As nature's critters gather round.
With buzzing bees and croaking songs,
They celebrate where laughter belongs.

So fling your worries far away,
In this sunny world, let's dance and sway.
For in the warmth of every ray,
The whispers of joy will always stay.

Threads of Twilight

In twilight's thread, we weave our tales,
With giggles soft, like tiny gales.
The berries blush in purple hues,
They tickle noses and steal your shoes.

The sun dips low, its laughter bright,
As shadows dance in fading light.
A squirrel's grin, a playful chase,
Together weaving this silly space.

With sticky hands and berry stains,
We slip and slide in nature's lanes.
Each berry plucked, a secret shared,
A puzzling fruit: are we prepared?

So come join in, with hearty cheer,
We'll berry-pick without a fear.
For in this twilight, we shall find,
A funny tale that's sweetly kind.

Harvest Harmony

In fields of green, we skip and shout,
As harvest time begins to sprout.
Beneath the leaves, a wobbly dance,
With berries bright, we take our chance.

A clumsy stumble, a jarring fall,
Oh, how we laugh, we can't recall!
The laughter rings, the sunlight glows,
As berry juice drips from our toes.

The pets join in, a merry sight,
Spinning 'round with sheer delight.
Sticky paws and tails a-fluff,
This berry picking's quite the stuff!

So let's embrace this berry spree,
With laughter sweet as jam on tea.
For in this harvest, we find bliss,
In every giggle, in every miss.

Nature's Sweetest Verse

In nature's arms, we seek a rhyme,
Where berries tangle like old chimes.
With twigs as quills, we scribble fun,
From dawn till dusk, we've just begun.

With every pick, our laughter swells,
The ants remind us of their spells.
We twirl and trip, a merry mess,
Creativity in chaos, no less!

With berry hats atop our heads,
We prance around like silly threads.
The birds all giggle, the bees hum tunes,
While we compose our silly croons.

In hues of red and shades of blue,
We find a joy, so pure and true.
Nature's sweetest verse, we sing,
The berry heart's delightful fling.

Echoes from the Green

In the quiet woods, the laughter echoes,
As we collide with leafy meadows.
With berry crowns and beaming grins,
Nature's laughter, it always wins.

We stomp through leaves, a playful thud,
In search of treasure, sweet as bud.
The bushes rustle, a faint surprise,
As giggling critters roll their eyes.

With colors bright, we paint the scene,
Our berry mischief becomes a dream.
Each sticky bite, a moment shared,
In fun and folly, we are ensnared.

So heed the echoes, let them flow,
In every giggle, let laughter grow.
For in the green, where shadows play,
We find the joy in every day.

Scented Paths

In the garden where the laughter grows,
Wobbling gnomes on their tippy toes,
A taste of jam on the breeze does play,
Chasing bees who flit away.

Squirrel's dance in a goofy fray,
Tripping over a berry buffet,
Giggles burst like bubbles wide,
As clumsy critters take a ride.

Fragrant trails, oh what a sight,
Hedgehogs spin in a dizzy flight,
Berry stains on tails so bright,
Nature's joke—oh what delight!

In this patch of playful cheer,
Each laugh, each squawk, we hold so dear,
With sticky fingers, we will share,
This joyful dance, beyond compare.

The Bower of Shadows

Underneath the leafy gloom,
Rabbits plot a berry bloom,
Whispered tales of strawberry pie,
Spinning yarns as the fireflies fly.

The old owl hoots a silly rhyme,
Saying 'Just once, do it for a dime!'
Berries tumble, higgledy-piggledy,
Dancing shadows, oh how they jiggle-y!

A raccoon tries to nap on a branch,
While wearing pajamas—what a chance!
The ripest fruit falls with a thud,
Covered in giggles and a bit of mud.

In the twilight's soft embrace,
Every berry finds its place,
A bower's laughter wraps around,
Joyful echoes, sweetly found.

The Fruitful Hour

At dusk, the fruits begin to sing,
Bouncing notes on a bouncy spring,
Lemon drops, each with a grin,
Swaying gently, let the fun begin!

The peaches hold a grand parade,
While naughty cherries hatch a trade,
Plum pie wishes float on air,
With whispers sweet that we all share.

A debate on which is the best,
Raspberries say, 'We're not like the rest!'
The blackberries laugh with a spiky pride,
As the zestful fruits gather side by side.

Oh, fruity revels on this spree,
Nature's fun, come share with me,
An hour of joy beneath the stars,
With laughter echoing near and far.

Nature's Juicy Confessions

A grape confessed to an orange bright,
'I'm feeling squishy, is that all right?'
The blueberries giggled, all in a row,
'This juicy secret, let it flow!'

Under vines of the wild green,
Fruits spill secrets, oh what a scene!
In the spotlight, a mango winks,
While the cactus chimes in with gentle jinks.

'You can't out-sweet me!' a ripe plum said,
Puffing out juice that made folks dread,
But the pineapple laughed, all spiky and bold,
'Your sapphire charm is getting old!'

In this orchard of chatty delight,
Each fruity laugh brings pure respite,
As nature spills the rhymes we adore,
Juicy confessions, forevermore.

Melodies in the Meadow

In the meadow where giggles bloom,
Bouncing berries spell out a tune,
Silly squirrels join in the dance,
While rabbits hop in a bright prance.

A pigeon perched on a clumsy vine,
Whistles out a rhythm, oh so fine,
Caterpillars sway with all their might,
As fireflies blink in the fading light.

A hedgehog wears a hat too big,
Struts about like a funky dig,
With every twist, he trips and rolls,
The berries on his dance floor strolls.

So join the fun, don't be a grouch,
Bring your friends for a good ol' slouch,
In the meadow where laughter flows,
Nature's chorus is how it goes.

A Tangle of Dreams

In a garden wild and steep,
Berries whisper secrets, oh so deep,
A squirrel dreams of a berry feast,\nWhile a hedgehog plots to be the least.

Bumblebees buzz with a silly sound,
Word of mischief that's spread around,
They fling the fruit as if to tease,
While laughter tickles the tall green trees.

A rabbit debates with a flower's head,
Whose berry pie should be widespread,
The flower brags, "My recipe's swell,"
While the rabbit rolls eyes, "Oh, do tell!"

A tangle of dreams in every nook,
Stories inspire with every look,
With giggles bouncing off the leaves,
A place of fun where joy never leaves.

Gem-Laden Branches

Look up high at the gem-filled sights,
Branches hang low with berry delights,
A pigeon's dive, a daring swoop,
Turns into a messy berry scoop.

A grumpy cat stuck on a limb,
Grabs a raspberry, takes a whim,
"Who knew," it puffs with juices bright,
"Being berry drunk feels so right!"

With each plop, the laughter grows,
As friends below dodge berry throws,
A mouse in a hat joins in the toss,
Claiming victory, "Look at this gloss!"

Chasing colors in shades so bold,
Natures mischief, a sight to behold,
Gem-laden branches, so full of cheer,
A fruity fest that brings us near.

Harvest Moon's Caress

Under the harvest moon's warm embrace,
Berries shimmer in a joyful race,
Bouncing across the field of gold,
With tales of sweet mischief to be told.

A raccoon sneaks a little taste,
With a furry band that can't be placed,
They giggle and tumble with every bite,
While the moon winks at the comical sight.

Crickets conduct an offbeat band,
As foxes join with a berry in hand,
The dance gets wild as twilight descends,
A merry chaos that never ends.

With cheeks all stained and hearts so light,
They celebrate a berry feast tonight,
Under the moon's caress, we play,
In laughter and joy, come what may.

A Dance of Sweetness

In the garden where giggles bloom,
Little critters scamper and zoom.
Berries plop in baskets of cheer,
While squirrels join in, swaying near.

With every step, a stumble and fall,
The jolly old rabbit performs for all.
He twirls with flair, a sight to see,
While the birds chuckle, chirping with glee.

A fruit feast under a lopsided tree,
As llamas wear hats, how silly they be!
A dance of laughter fills up the air,
With every berry, worries they scare.

So come join the fun, don't be a fuss,
In this patch of joy, each laugh's a plus.
In this wild party, the fruits all sway,
With sweet jams made from happy play!

Dark Red and Dusk

In the fields, colors blend and swirl,
Dark red berries twirl and whirl.
Under a sky painted with dreams,
Giggling as the moonlight gleams.

The owls wear glasses, looking quite wise,
While rabbits play poker under the skies.
Each berry plucked is a giggly surprise,
With each pop, the laughter flies!

The sunset spills juice, a sticky delight,
While raccoons dance into the night.
Their wiggly tails sing a silly song,
In this twilight, nothing feels wrong.

As stars sprinkle laughter in the deep blue,
The critters toast to the evening's woohoo!
With dark red splashes on paws and snouts,
In this twilight, funny dreams sprout!

The Secret Softness

Whispers of sweetness hide in the brush,
Where berries giggle in a jolly hush.
The secret softness brings joy anew,
With fluffy clouds that give a due.

Beneath the leaves, mushrooms with hats,
Jive with the beetles, and dance with the cats.
A wiggly worm wears a shiny bow,
As they strut in the twinkle of the flow.

The breeze carries chuckles from tall trees,
While hedgehogs roll with the greatest of ease.
A bubble of laughter fills up the space,
In this secret grove, with a charming grace.

So gather around for the giggles and fun,
In the warmth of the sun, we dance and run.
With berries so sweet and friends aplenty,
In the secret softness, life is friendly.

Harvesting Dreams

Under the sun where the laughter grows,
Dreams are harvested, as everyone knows.
The baskets overflow with giggles and cheer,
While the forest joins in with a silly sneer.

The frogs wear boots and skip with delight,
As the grasshoppers leap into the night.
Each splat of a fruit sings a merry tune,
As the night dances under the playful moon.

Berry stains on paws tell tales untold,
As the critters gather in the evening bold.
With stories of sweetness and laughter so bright,
The spirit of joy is a dazzling sight.

So come one, come all, for a dream-filled spree,
In this patch of whimsy, there's magic to see.
As we harvest the dreams with each silly shout,
In the fields of laughter, there's never a doubt!

Orchard Murmurs

In the orchard, apples grin,
Chasing squirrels, let the fun begin.
Peaches dance, they twirl around,
Laughing softly, such joy is found.

Lemons hang, with sour faces,
Winking at the playful chases.
Cherries giggle, red and round,
Daring birds to come on down.

Grapes plot mischief in their vines,
Hiding secrets, sipping wines.
Ripe and sweet, they coax with cheer,
Join the party, come on dear!

So in this grove, let laughter bloom,
With fruit so sweet, the world's a room.
Together we'll spin tales so bright,
Under sun and starlit night.

Rustic Rhymes

In fields where wildflowers play,
Bees hum tunes in bright array.
Frogs in hats jump on the scene,
Ribbiting rhythms, oh so keen!

Tomatoes wearing boots of red,
Strut their stuff, you should be fed.
Radishes rock in funky grooves,
Shaking roots, they've got the moves!

Corn stalks whisper silly jokes,
While carrots giggle, poking folks.
Nothing here is ever bland,
Join us, take a veggie stand!

With every laugh, the sun shall shine,
In this patch, all is divine.
Rustic tales and rhymes so fine,
Planted deep in heart and vine.

Twilight in the Briar Patch

As twilight gleams on thorny trails,
Bramble critters tell their tales.
Bunnies bounce with silly grace,
While hedgehogs giggle, just in place.

Fireflies twinkle like little stars,
Dancing 'round with glowing jars.
Raccoons drum on the old fence post,
A midnight show that we love most.

Berries blush in shades of night,
Seizing moments, pure delight.
Squirrels spin yarns of daring feats,
While crickets play their buzzing beats.

In this patch where mischief reigns,
Laughter echoes, joy sustains.
So gather near, let spirits rise,
In the briar patch beneath the skies.

Sips of Summer Starlight

In summer's glow, we sip and scheme,
Lemonade pops bursting with cream.
Melons blend in a fruity duel,
Watermelons splash, our summer fuel.

Shortcakes stack with layers high,
Strawberries laugh, oh me, oh my!
Whipped cream clouds in the bright sun,
Tasting chaos, oh, what fun!

Pineapples dance, their tops a crown,
Sending giggles all around.
Grapefruit throws a zesty jest,
With every sip, we are so blessed.

So raise a glass to summer skies,
With laughter here, joy never dies.
In every sip, let spirit glide,
Under starlight, we shall bide.

Treading Through Tender Flesh

A squirrel in socks, what a sight,
He dances on roots, oh what might!
With berries as shoes, he skips with glee,
While snickering leaves shout, "Look at me!"

A toe in the mud, he slips and slides,
Laughing so hard, he nearly collides!
A foolish frog joins the fun in the stream,
Their antics make nature burst at the seam.

A raccoon plays drums on an old tin can,
Inventing a jig with his very own plan.
With berries as maracas, they shake and jive,
While the trees sway like they're happily alive.

The sun sets low, painting skies bright,
Each critter now gathered for a dance at night.
In tender terrain, laughter does thrive,
Where silly shenanigans keep joy alive.

Whimsy in the Wilderness

A hedgehog in glasses sits up on a stump,
Reading a map, oh what a chump!
He wanders from trail, lost in his book,
While all of his friends just giggle and look.

A rabbit in boots leaps over a log,
Chasing a rather confused old dog.
With each little hop and twist of his tail,
He shouts, "Let's go, we cannot fail!"

A parrot gets busy, painting bright stones,
Creating a rainbow, she's lost in her tones.
Nature's own colors all blend and gleam,
As critters take part in her wild, wacky dream.

The night sings a tune with the stars up above,
While the raccoon and owl share secrets of love.
Laughter rings out, nothing serious in sight,
In this wild, whimsical, heartfelt delight.

The Curve of a Petal

A ladybug lounges, dressed to impress,
With polka-dot flair, she's a true fashion mess!
She sips on sweet nectar, what a delight,
While worms roll their eyes, thinking, "What a sight!"

A bumblebee boogies, all wiggly and bold,
Whispering secrets to blossoms so old.
With petals a-twirl, they dance in the breeze,
While ants form a line, working with ease.

The sunbeams come down, the flowers go 'pop',
In colors so vivid, you just can't stop!
With all of their giggles, the garden does sigh,
As butterflies flutter and then bravely fly.

A grasshopper strums on a leaf for a beat,
While everyone gathers to dance on their feet.
In the curve of a petal, joy never fails,
A light-hearted story with giggles and tales.

Nature's Hidden Choir

In the glade, there's a croak, and a chirp and a laugh,
The frogs are all singing, they're done with the math!
With crickets and owls, they form quite a band,
Each note a reminder, that life's truly grand.

A chipmunk on tambourine, shiny and round,
Keeps rhythm while starlings fly all around.
They've gathered their friends for a concert tonight,
With nature's own sounds, oh what a delight!

The willows sway softly, they join in the song,
While foxes and rabbits all dance along.
The night is a party with smiles all around,
As laughter and music through the woods sound!

As moonlight spills down, there's magic in play,
With critters united, they finish the day.
Nature's choir sings sweet, in harmony clear,
Their melody echoes, bringing joy and cheer.

Petals and Laughter in the Glade

In the sunlight's glow, they prance and play,
Frogs in tuxedos jumping a ballet.
Daisies giggle, and vines entwine,
As the bees buzz tunes, sweet as wine.

Squirrels wear hats made of leaf and twig,
Dancing 'round pillars, a wobbly jig.
The rose had a jest, oh what a hoot,
Telling tales of the dancing root!

The clouds burst forth in laughter's cheer,
Tickling each flower, buzzing so near.
With petals that swirl in the joyous breeze,
It's a fruity fiesta, if you please!

At dusk, fireflies twinkle, a sparkling sight,
The garden's a stage, bathed in twilight.
Amid giggles and grins, the fun doubles,
In this wacky world of nature's cuddles.

Poem of the Restless Forager

A critter with pockets, oh what a sight,
Hoarding summer's bounty, oh what delight!
Grapes in his hat, a peach in his paw,
Off to the grove, with no time to draw.

He stops for a snack, a berry or two,
But tripped on a root, flew into the blue!
Landed in a patch where the jam jars greet,
In a sticky quandary, now this is sweet!

The jam making critters all begin to cheer,
As he rolls on the ground, squashing those spheres.
Laughter erupts; it's a culinary plight,
With blueberry splatters painting the night!

With berries as hats, they sing a loud tune,
Under the watch of the cheeky moon.
For in that shenanigan, friendship is born,
In the wild and the jam, where joy is adorned.

Melodies from the Vine-Covered Arbour

In an arbour where laughter flows like a stream,
The crickets compose their sweet little theme.
Twinkling notes bounce from moon to the floor,
While shadows of vines dance forevermore.

A grape sang a song, so plump in its plight,
"Join me, dear friends, in this zesty night!"
With kazooing frogs and a clarinet bee,
Their music rang out, a wild jubilee.

But then came a thud, a sneeze and a shout,
The band was disrupted, oh what a rout!
A squirrel with swagger stole grapes in a flash,
While the hedgehogs all giggled, enjoying the crash.

Under the stars, the revelers spun,
Dancing to rhythms 'til morning begun.
With laughter and jests, the arbour is bright,
In melodies shared, all turns out just right!

The Shaded Feast of Summer's End

Under the boughs, where the sunlight has fled,
The critters prepare for a feast, oh so spread!
Cherries and melons stacked high on each plate,
The aroma of laughter, it beckons so great.

The raccoon with style dons a bright yellow tie,
Serving up cocktails, oh my, oh my!
While chipmunks debate on the best berry pie,
A slippery joke - watch the sour owl fly!

As friends gather round for this whimsical cheer,
The feast becomes chaos, as mischief draws near.
With a splash of fruit punch, a splatter of zest,
Each critter will sip from the berry-juice fest.

With stories and giggles, the hours move fast,
Recalling the summer, oh how it will last.
In the shade of the trees, all is merry and bright,
For this end-of-season brings laughter and light!

Hidden Treasures in the Woodland Shadows

In the woods where critters hide,
Lurking treasures sit inside.
A squirrel with a grin so wide,
Hoarded berries, oh what a ride!

With every bite, my face turns red,
Chasing shadows, care to spread?
A berry here, a berry there,
Giggles float upon the air.

The rabbits laugh, the hedgehogs cheer,
Hiding goodies, oh so near!
But watch your step, don't trip in glee,
Or give all the snacks away to me!

Every turn's a sweet delight,
As woodland wonders take their flight.
Among the leaves and playful moles,
Hidden treasures, oh how it rolls!

Tales Woven in Tangy Color

In a patch where colors blend,
Fruity tales have no end.
Blue and red, they twist and twine,
A raucous chorus, how divine!

A rogue raccoon sings a tune,
While berries jive beneath the moon.
Splat! The juice on hats aplenty,
A berry mess — oh, it's quite trendy!

These goblins giggle as they dash,
Through wonderlands of berry bash.
Lemonade rain serves to quench,
As laughter echoes from every bench!

Tales are spun with every bite,
Fruity tales, both day and night.
Berries dance and goblins shout,
In tangle of colors, there's no doubt!

Captured by the Fragrance of June

June arrives with scents so sweet,
Berries bloom beneath my feet.
A dainty snack, or so it seems,
Whispers float in fruity dreams!

A snicker here, a burble there,
Nature's laughter fills the air.
Bumblebees play hide and seek,
As berry lovers reach their peak!

Amid the vines with charming smell,
The pungent bounty casts a spell.
What joy to nibble on nature's cake,
Yet watch out, don't make a mistake!

For squirrels plot with craft and flair,
To steal the treasures we all share.
In June's embrace so bold and bright,
We twirl through flavors, pure delight!

The Dance of the Midnight Pickers

Under stars that brightly twink,
We gather snacks while the world winks.
A moonlit dance, a berry spree,
With giggles bursting, wild and free!

Clumsy feet and berry stains,
Squeezed between the joyful reins.
Pickers tiptoe, slip, and slide,
In the thrill of night, no need to hide!

Raccoon dances, caught in glee,
While fireflies buzz along the spree.
A wild serenade begins to swell,
As midnight pickers weave their spell!

With every basket filled to the brim,
Laughter echoes on a silly whim.
So join the brawl, don't hesitate,
For night-time fruits, oh, they await!

Pippin and Poem

In the garden red and round,
Pippin danced, the sweetest sound.
He tickled each ripe little berry,
Singing songs, oh so merry!

With a hop and a skip, he'd leap,
A squirrel watched, began to creep.
Pippin's hat flew, caught a bird,
The chaos spread, it was absurd!

He plucked a fruit to make a jam,
But missed the jar, it was a sham.
The kitchen turned into a fight,
With sticky laughter, pure delight!

So come and join the berry fun,
Bring your friends, let's all run.
With Pippin's smile and silly schemes,
Life is sweeter than our dreams!

A Tapestry of Tastes

Colors bright in summer's lap,
A tapestry in nature's map.
Each berry burst, a taste to share,
With giggles floating in the air.

Jack the clown with purple stains,
Adventured forth, with berry gains.
He wore a crown of tangled vines,
Drawing laughs with funny lines!

Sally's pie was quite the sight,
With wiggles, jigs, and sheer delight.
But as she served, the pie took flight,
And hit the dog, oh what a sight!

So gather round the patch today,
Find the laughter, let it stay.
With juicy fruits and silly tales,
Life's a feast where joy prevails!

Shades of Autumn's Kiss

Autumn leaves with colors bright,
Wear a crown by morning light.
Berries glisten in the breeze,
Pico in a dance with ease!

With a chuckle and a twirl,
Pico spun like a merry whirl.
The dog surprised, ran in the way,
And sent him sliding, oh what play!

Neighbors peek with laughter loud,
As Pico lands, he's quite the cloud.
Chubby cheeks, and berry stains,
Who knew fun could wear such chains?

So gather 'round, laugh with glee,
In every berry, joy's decree.
Autumn's kiss in every bite,
Brings out the funny, pure delight!

The Sweetness Between Thorns

Roses red and thorns up high,
Berries hiding, oh my oh my!
Lila laughed, her hands all green,
A treasure hunt like never seen!

With sticky fingers, muddled glee,
She danced around the bumblebee.
But oh! A thorn gave a little poke,
Her laughter mixed with a silly choke!

Picking berries, what a game,
Spilling juice, should be a shame.
Yet in the mess, she felt so free,
Life's little joys, a sweet decree!

So cherish moments, between the thorns,
With laughter, joy, and playful scorns.
For in the patches, wild and bold,
Lie memories worth more than gold!

Rhapsody of Ripe Delights

In the garden where laughter grows,
Fruits are dancing, striking poses.
Cherries giggle, plump and round,
While blueberries bounce upon the ground.

Grapes in clusters, spinning tales,
With wobbly legs, they tip and scale.
Raspberry whispers, 'Let's play a game!'
While strawberries tease with juicy fame.

The rhubarb winks, it knows the score,
Gossiping sweetly by the orchard door.
In this merry parade of delight,
The fruits are revelers, day and night.

So grab a basket, join the cheer,
In this fruity frolic, bring your gear.
With laughter ripening on each vine,
The harvest of humor is truly divine.

Thicket Serenade

In the thicket where giggles sprout,
Wild fruits whisper their secret routes.
A plum in a polka dot dress,
Sings to a peach, 'This is our mess!'

The blackberries bounce, a rowdy crew,
'Join us!' they shout, 'We'll paint you blue!'
While lemons chuckle with a zesty cheer,
'We'll squeeze out laughter; come gather near!'

Nuts with suits, ever so sly,
Crack jokes that make the squirrels cry.
Each leaf a laugh, each stem a jam,
The thicket's a stage, oh, what a slam!

So gather your friends and take a seat,
In this thicket of fun, you can't be beat.
For nature's tales are the best we know,
With a splash of humor, let's have a show!

Songs of the Wild Fruit

Beneath the sun where wild fruits sing,
Laughing loudly of the joy they bring.
Apples joke about their red cheer,
While figs flip-flop with no hint of fear.

Peaches are prancing in sunny delight,
As melons roll left, then dash to the right.
'Come join our party!' bursts forth the pears,
While cherries climb trees, flaunting their airs.

The elderberry's wisdom is full of glee,
With stories of mischief from old rascally.
Currants chirp in high sprite-like tunes,
While nuts play drums beneath the full moon.

Sing along with the wild and free,
In the orchard of fun, there's joy to see.
Let nature's laughter brighten your day,
As we dance with fruits in a merry ballet!

The Hidden Orchard's Echo

In a hush of leaves, where mischief lurks,
The hidden orchard's fruit jumps and jerks.
A kiwi whispers a riddle, quite funny,
While a nutty acorn dreams of honey.

Bananas slide, doing the twist,
Claiming, 'We're the best, don't get us missed!'
Watermelons revel in splashy delight,
With each juicy joke taking flight.

Peppers giggle in their little coats,
Running around like cheerful goats.
Sassy lemons squeeze out the punch,
Fire up the fun with a fruity brunch!

So tiptoe slow, hear the echoes play,
In this hidden orchard, laughter's the way.
With fruits as friends, feel the joy unfold,
In this secret haven of stories untold.

Secrets in the Shrubbery

In a thicket where laughter grows,
A squirrel sings and a robin knows.
Chasing shadows, they leap with glee,
While bushes hide secrets, wild and free.

A hedgehog waltz in a dizzy spin,
With berries bouncing on his chin.
He twirls around in a frantic hop,
As the fruits all giggle, they just can't stop.

The bushes whisper tales of cheer,
Of hidden stash that draw us near.
With branches waving, they tease and play,
Inviting all to join the fray.

So come along, don't be so shy,
In the shrubbery where joy can fly.
With every step, let laughter rise,
In this leafy land where fun belies.

The Berry-Laced Path

On a path marked by jammy trails,
A raccoon giggles, the laughter sails.
With sticky paws and berry-stained face,
He trips on tales of a wild-goose chase.

Beneath a tree, a gnome sits tight,
His belly full, his grin a sight.
He swipes at berries that bounce and roll,
As critters gather to fill their bowl.

A ghostly fog of fruity zest,
Leaves all the critters feeling blessed.
With every berry, a chuckle ensues,
On this winding road, one can't lose.

So find your slice of that merry way,
Where silliness reigns both night and day.
Feel every squish, embrace the laugh,
On this berry-laced, fun-hearted path.

Sunlit Interludes

In sunlit gaps where shadows play,
A rabbit grins, come join the fray.
With skippy hops and a cheeky flick,
He juggles berries, what a neat trick!

Chickadees chirp a melody bright,
As sunbeams dance with pure delight.
Berries tumble like laughter in air,
Each roll and bounce beyond compare.

A lizard slides with a silly grin,
Where joy is found, there's no chagrin.
Fruits and fun come hand in hand,
In this sunny, sweetened land.

So wander down, let spirits lift,
In interludes where joys are gift.
With laughter packed in every ray,
Sunlit moments make the day.

Aroma of Abundance

In the garden where aromas flare,
The scent of mischief whispers in air.
With strawberries ripe, secrets unfold,
A tasting spree, relentless and bold.

A bear in shades takes a fruity bite,
His grin so wide, what a funny sight.
He roars with glee, spills juice on the ground,
While critters laugh, a spectacle found.

Follow the scent, skip and swirl,
A thrilling waltz in a berry whirl.
With each delicious, juicy smack,
We dance through laughter, never look back.

So lift a cup to this lavish show,
Where the aroma of abundance doth glow.
With every berry, a giggle ignites,
In this bountiful spree, our joy ignites.

Sweetness in the Thorns

In the garden, berries gleam,
Hiding secrets, oh what a dream!
But beware of prickly foes,
They tickle toes and poke your nose!

A squirrel dances with great flair,
Stealing snacks without a care.
While I sip on wild fruit tea,
He plots to steal it all from me!

The raccoons join the merry crew,
Shaking branches, berries flew!
Amidst the laughter and the mess,
We find sweet joy and soft distress!

So let's all feast in this bright dell,
Where thorns and giggles weave a spell!
With sticky fingers, hearts ablaze,
We'll sing our tune in berry haze!

The Secret Grove

In the grove where giggles sprout,
We dance around, we twist about!
With every berry in our hand,
We form a wild, berry band!

An owl hoots from high above,
While squirrels tease with merry love.
The bushes rustle, secrets spill,
As laughter echoes, loud and shrill!

Whispers dance on leafy air,
With hidden treasures everywhere.
We pluck and munch with silly grins,
While nature laughs at all our sins!

So come along, you berry band,
With sticky palms, let's take a stand!
In the grove where we all play,
We find our fun in a wondrous way!

Starlit Gatherings

Under a sky that's oh so bright,
We gather 'round in pure delight.
With moonlit berries on a plate,
We laugh and dance; it's truly great!

The fireflies join in with their glow,
As we tell tales that start to flow.
We munch on fruits with silly cheer,
While rhymes and jingles fill the sphere!

A billy goat comes to steal our pie,
With slyness in his hungry eye.
But quick as lightning, we shoo him away,
And continue our fun without delay!

So raise your voices, let them soar,
In starlit gatherings, we want more!
With nature's bounty on our lips,
Our laughter echoes, joy never slips!

Nectar on the Breeze

The flowers open wide and bright,
As buzzing bees take their flight.
They share their nectar, sweet and bold,
While stories of their travels unfold!

A toasty sun warms up our day,
While froggy jumps make quite a play.
With syrupy fruits all around,
Our giggles bounce without a sound!

The silly ants march in a line,
Carrying treats, oh how they shine!
But watch your step, they may just swarm,
And turn our picnic into a storm!

So let's enjoy this breezy feast,
With laughter in our hearts, at least!
For nothing beats a day like this,
With nectar dreams and berry bliss!

Harmonies of Nature's Bounty

In the garden where fruits take flight,
Cherries wink at the stars at night.
Raspberries giggle in the warm sunlight,
And the strawberries dance with pure delight.

Bees buzz in a honeyed song,
While the plump peaches hum along.
Blueberries chuckle, feeling bold,
As nature's treasures unfold like gold.

The playful vines twist and twine,
Each grape a jester, dressed so fine.
Lemons laugh with a zesty cheer,
Turning frowns into smiles near and dear.

As the day fades and colors blend,
Fruits unite, their laughter won't end.
When harvest comes, it's a fruit parade,
With nature's bounty, all worries fade.

Echoes of the Harvest Moon

Under the moon, fruits shine so bright,
Apples whisper secrets of night.
Pears serenade with sweet refrains,
While figs exchange their silly gains.

Cider spills tales of laughter shared,
Plums plop down without a care.
The harvest dances, it's quite a sight,
With fruits and critters, oh what a night!

The pumpkins chuckle, looking round,
Telling jokes that are truly profound.
As owls hoot and the night grows bold,
Nature sings stories, which never get old.

So savor the echoes under the moon,
In the orchards where the laughter is strewn.
With every bite, a giggle or two,
Harvest time fun—just me and you.

A Tangy Serenade at Dusk

As twilight wraps the day in zest,
Lemons laugh, feeling truly blessed.
Grapefruits wear hats of tangy cheer,
Singing sweet songs that all want to hear.

Peaches are blushing, don't be shy,
They spin in circles, oh my, oh my!
Kiwi's juggling in a playful way,
While berries join in the wild ballet.

At dusk, the fruits share their dreams,
Melons plop and burst at the seams.
With every crunch, a funny tale,
Of fruity quests and mischievous trails.

As stars twinkle in a laughing spree,
Nature's bounty brings joy and glee.
It's a tangy serenade we hold dear,
With every bite, we toast and cheer!

Rhythm of the Ripened Sun

In the sun's warm embrace, fruits sway and spin,
Watermelons chuckle as the day begins.
Bananas sing low, on their leafy throne,
While oranges bounce, in a fruity tone.

The rhythm's a giggle, a juicy refrain,
Pineapples stomp, shaking off the rain.
Tangerines tinkle like bells in a choir,
Each bite a laugh as we dance in the mire.

The harvest comes with a playful wink,
Tomatoes blush as their juices link.
Every fruit's a dancer, wild and free,
In nature's cabaret, just you and me.

So let's toast the day with laughter bright,
As the ripened sun bids us goodnight.
In the garden of giggles, join the fun,
Where every fruit sparkles, kissed by the sun.

Illuminated by the Wild's Sweetness

In the thicket, fruit hangs low,
Chasing critters, it's quite the show.
A squirrel slips, wearing jam stains,
As laughter echoes through the lanes.

Beneath the sun, the vines will sway,
While bees join in their buzzing play.
A raccoon with a pie-shaped face,
Is plotting treats with such fine grace.

The children dance like fireflies,
Waving sticks, giggles in the skies.
Each berry pluck invites a cheer,
As sticky fingers draw us near.

So gather round, let's fill our cups,
With juice that spills and funny ups.
We'll sing of fruits and silly games,
'Neath wild sweetness, no one shames.

Fables of Flora and Fruition

In tangled greens, where mischief grows,
The fruits spin tales that nobody knows.
A plump blue orb starts telling lies,
While questioning all the other pies.

A bushy tale, quite tall it seems,
When carrots argue over dreams.
Strawberries chuckle, rubbing their seeds,
While counting stems like fancy beads.

The gnomes are up to sneaky tricks,
In pinstripe suits, collecting picks.
A wise old sage, a pear-shaped chap,
Snoozes soundly, lost in a nap.

When dusk arrives, and laughs collide,
The fruits unite for nightly pride.
With every giggle, tales ignite,
In the chaos of the moonlit night.

Voices of the Canopy's Gemstones

In leafy crowns, the berries gleam,
Each gem a part of nature's dream.
A parrot squawks, its laughter bright,
As oranges drop in a silly flight.

The wild vines twist, they dance on air,
They sway and twirl without a care.
A mouse in boots takes quite the leap,
With fruity dreams that make us weep.

Tall trees gossip, with whispers sweet,
A chatty trunk spills secrets neat.
Fungi giggle, it's a sight,
Bringing colors to the balmy night.

So gather 'round, let hearts be light,
In the canopy's enchanting night.
With fruit-filled stories in the wind,
The joy of nature shall not end.

The Taste of Wind's Whispers

The wind carries laughter through the glade,
As scents of fruit bring light to shade.
A lazy bee starts telling jokes,
With honey dips and giggling folks.

Cherries blush, they're feeling bold,
With whispers sweet and tales retold.
A playful breeze tugs at your hat,
As ducks in line go splat, splat, splat!

The grasshoppers dance, trying their best,
While everyone else takes a rest.
With every munch, a wink is shared,
For fruity humor, we've all dared.

As twilight casts its gentle hues,
We toast with cups of fruit-filled views.
In every laugh, the night confides,
The sweet taste of nature's joyful rides.

The Chorus Beneath the Canopy

Under the leaves a chorus does sing,
Squirrels dance wildly, imagining spring.
With acorns as trumpets, they play their tune,
While chipmunks perform, strumming stars and the moon.

Laughter erupts from the high branches sway,
As birds chirp a jingle, in their own little way.
Nuts rolling down in a nutty ballet,
The forest's a stage for a wacky display.

Raccoons juggle berries, oh what a sight,
With mischief abounding; they're quite out of plight.
The trees echo giggles, the ground shakes with cheer,
Nature's own spectacle, it's all crystal clear!

So raise up a toast to this fantastical show,
With laughter and joy, let the good times flow.
Beneath the tall canopy, friends both furry and bright,
Sing along with the forest, from morning till night.

Flavors of Forgotten Dreams

Once I tasted clouds, sweet like a kiss,
Melting on tongue with a sugary bliss.
But reality struck in a tangy surprise,
A pickle parade danced before my eyes.

I thought I'd roam fields of ice cream afloat,
With flavors of green grass and jellybean boat.
But along came a squirrel, claiming his prize,
With nuts all around, oh what a disguise!

We whipped up a potion, a stew from the past,
Cabbage and cream, mixed with pop rocks so fast.
A feast for the silly, that fled from the night,
In this playful kitchen, everything felt right.

So let us embrace this whimsical tease,
With flavors of laughter and funky unease.
In dreams, we can swirl, swirl, twirl, and scheme,
Together we'll savor this outlandish theme!

The Sweetest Symphony

In a grove of giggles, the berries all hum,
A symphony of sweetness, oh let's all come!
The blueberries blast with a bouncy delight,
While strawberries soft serenade through the night.

Raspberries tickle as they slide down the vines,
Each note full of mischief, as laughter entwines.
A cacophony of colors, so rich and so bright,
Healthiest concert, playing all through the night!

The juice flows like music, sticky yet sweet,
We dance in the rhythm, with skipping heartbeats.
The flaxen sun dips, as the stars start to twirl,
And each berry's a part of this magical whirl.

Join in with the fun, let your laughter ring,
For life's gentle melody is what we all sing.
In this fruity fantasia, so wild and so true,
The sweetest symphony, crafted for you!

Harvesting Heartstrings

Pluck the smiles from trees, they're ripe for the take,
Jars full of giggles, a chuckle earthquake.
With each tiny berry, a story unfolds,
Of whimsical wishes and secrets retold.

Gather the laughter, in baskets of cheer,
Where mischief is plenty, and friends are held dear.
Each heartstring we harvest, a tune that it plays,
The melody of friendship, in humorous ways.

With fingers all stained from the colors of fun,
Let's create sweet wonders under the sun.
A splash of wild juice, oh what a delight,
As moonbeams and giggles twirl into the night!

So here's to the moments we cherish and cling,
To the songs that we dance to, like birds on the wing.
In this garden of joy, let your spirit take flight,
For harvesting heartstrings makes everything right!

www.ingramcontent.com/pod-product-compliance
Lightning Source LLC
Chambersburg PA
CBHW071854160426
43209CB00003B/556